DAM IT!

Negotiating at the River's Edge

Tom Gosselin

For information contact tom@practicalnegotiating.com

Book and Cover design by Steve Gladstone

Illustration by K. B. Allen

ISBN: 978-1-7344872-0-6

First Edition: February, 2020

Contents

Foreword

As long as there have been people (and probably as long as there have been beavers!) there has been negotiation. Whether the contention is over division of scarce resources or status or who does the dishes, negotiation is the preferred process for reaching agreements that create value and avoid the damage – both tangible and emotional – that conflict engenders.

Although negotiation is an everyday occurrence, few people are as effective at is as they need to be.

The result? Opportunities for mutual benefit are lost and relationships suffer unnecessary damage.

The antidote is a good negotiation framework and a practical set of tools for applying it. But such a framework is best communicated not just through tables and charts and graphs, but through stories that illustrate the principles and provide people with the mental models they need to internalize and apply them.

This is what Tom Gosselin has accomplished with "Dam it". He has created a wonderful fable that tells the story of a classic conflict and how the right approach to negotiation resolved it. Readers will resonate to the many challenges facing the furry protagonists as they work their way through the forest and the trees to reach an equitable and sustainable solution. In the process they will learn what effective negotiating is really all about.

Michael Watkins – author of *The First 90 Days*

Dam It!

It's a frosty morning in late March and the sun is just peeking over the hills leading down to the river. "More water this year, lots of snow in the mountains," muses Bucky the beaver. With the heavy snowfall and an early spring thaw, the water flow on the river will be fast and furious in a month.

Over the last twenty odd years, Bucky and his family have been the only beavers in these woods. As a result, they could usually build or repair their dams at a leisurely pace and always had plenty of logs and branches left behind by the logging crews that regularly harvest along the river. Since his retirement as **Bucky Beaver**, a mascot for toothpaste[1], Bucky has been enjoying his kits[2] and their offspring. Recently, his kits moved away though, and he sees them just three or four times a year.

Over the course of the winter, Bucky's dam and lodge were severely damaged by excessive ice and snow. Now, Bucky has to build an entirely new dam and lodge, and the project seems daunting to him. He's got to move quickly before the full spring thaw. "Where can I find the energy to do this?" he ponders. As he's grown older his greying pelt has gotten thicker and his broad scaly tail has suffered damage from motorboat propellers.

---

[1] Bucky Beaver was the mascot of Ipana toothpaste in the '60s. Name used with permission of Maxill, Inc. St. Thomas, ON.

[2] Kits are the offspring of beavers.

Bucky heads back to his worksite and looks over the pile of timber he collected just yesterday. "Hmm, it seems I didn't bring as many logs and branches to the shore as I thought." Just then, he spies a trail left by the brush being pulled downstream. Bucky bristles and growls, "Who took my stuff?"

Bucky decides to follow the trail. A little more than half a mile down the river, he gets the odd feeling that he's not alone, maybe even that he is being watched. Over the years, his instincts have been sharpened against predators - animal and human. So, he is naturally suspicious.

As he enters a clearing, Bucky discovers some of the logs and branches that he collected just the other day. His distinctive teeth marks confirm that these are his branches. He's trying to figure out how the branches got this far down river. While he is pondering this mystery, he hears the distinctive chomping of a beaver's teeth nearby. Bucky is somewhat surprised since his has been the only beaver family on this river for as long as he can remember.

He decides to follow the sound. A little further into the woods, Bucky discovers the culprit. It's another beaver, younger and fitter than he. He hasn't been seen yet, so he has to decide whether to confront this beaver or to just retreat back upriver.

In the midst of his decision, the other beaver looks up somewhat startled and says, "Hey there, I didn't know there were any other beavers on this river."

Bucky decides to assert himself. "Yeah well, I've been on this river for 20 years and you took my branches and logs that I was planning to use for a new dam and lodge." The new younger beaver says, "Wow, I had no idea. I thought these branches were left over from the logging crew. My name is Hardy Beaver and I'm building a dam in this section of the river for my new family. I have new kits coming in the spring."

Bucky does not want a confrontation, but decides to state his position clearly, "Hold on there! I want to build **MY** dam on this river, and I've got seniority! I have to get working on it **NOW**."

Hardy is somewhat put off by this, but states firmly, "I'm young and I need to build a dam quickly to protect and raise my family. Besides, you're too old and slow to build a dam."

The two proud beavers begin a slow dance locking their eyes as if in battle. Bucky states, "Look here, Hardy, there can be only one dam on this river. Otherwise, the townspeople will come and break up both of our dams to keep the river flowing and avoid flooding the roadway. You'll just have to find another stream to build on."

Hardy retorts, "I have to build here, my mate is too pregnant for us to move to a different stream." Bucky begins to walk away. Hardy asserts, "Is that it? No more discussion?" Bucky stops and softens a bit saying, "Well, maybe I could help you find another stream." Hardy snaps, "Never mind, I'll find another stream. I don't need your help." and stomps off to find another stream.

After looking for several hours and over many miles, Hardy can't find a suitable stream. As the sun is setting, he heads home frustrated.

This whole day has been very frustrating. Ever since he moved from upriver, he's been looking for a suitable stream and now he's found it. Hardy had to move downriver because of trappers and hunters who had captured his father. He supposed that moving downstream and closer to town would be safer, and he could avoid being captured. As his new family is growing, he is anxious and fearful of not finding a suitable site and building his dam and lodge in time for the arrival of his kits.

Meanwhile, Bucky is gathering materials and beginning to lay the foundation of his dam. "Oh, this is a lot more work than the last time. Every task takes twice as long. I just don't have the energy I had ten years ago." He decides to quit for the day, and heads home exhausted.

Back upriver on the bank by his temporary lodge, Bucky Beaver is talking to his mate, Becky. "I ran into this other beaver who had the audacity to take my materials and start building a dam downriver. I'm pretty upset about it. You know we can't have two dams on the river." Becky says, "I didn't know there were any other beavers on the river. What kind of a beaver is he?" Bucky replies, "He's young and seems like a pretty straightforward fellow. He told me that his mate is pregnant with kits coming in the spring." He continues gruffly, "But, that doesn't change the fact that we have to have a new dam and lodge and we have seniority."

Becky says, "Let's think about this for a moment." She strokes Bucky's pelt and says, "Look how tired you are from working on the new dam, and you're just gathering materials at this point. I'm worried about you." Bucky is glum. Becky says, "You know, Bucky, you can be pretty hardheaded and gruff. It would be nice to have a new family on the river."

Further down the river, Hardy Beaver is telling his side of the story to his mate, Harriet. "He accused me of taking his stuff, and he thinks that he has seniority because he's old." Hardy continues, "He insisted I find another stream. I walked around for a couple of hours, and there aren't any other streams."

Harriet responds, "Sounds like a tough day. Tell me more about him."

Hardy describes Bucky as an old but pretty savvy beaver. "He seems to know what he's doing and has collected some great materials. And, he has amazingly strong teeth for a beaver his age."

"Well," Harriet replies, "I'd really like to meet him. Maybe we could all get together and come up with a solution."

Meanwhile, the Town Council is meeting about this very issue. The town controls the use of the river and whether or not the beavers can actually build a dam. When the Town Council noticed that there were two dams being built on the river, they planned to remove both; concerned that restricted water flow would flood the roadway. One of the members of the Town Council is an active environmentalist who often goes down to the river to sketch and paint. She was concerned that the Council would make a hasty decision to destroy both dams. She realizes the environmental advantage of having at least one dam on the river to facilitate water purification. She suggests that the Town Council members survey the river before making a final decision.

The very next day, Bucky and Becky head down river to the site of the new dam. As it turns out, Hardy and Harriet are sitting on a log in a clearing near the river enjoying the morning sunshine. Hardy and Bucky look at each other warily, and then walk off toward the river leaving their mates to get acquainted.

Hardy says, "I looked a couple of miles in each direction. There aren't any other streams. I don't know what to do."

Now that Bucky has heard about Hardy's frustrated search, he becomes more sympathetic and admits, "I guess I'm pretty hardheaded. I wanted to build this dam as a showpiece. It's probably my last dam, and I wanted it to be my legacy. But it's a big project and I hope I have the strength to finish it. Yesterday, I got started and went home absolutely exhausted."

Hardy decides to share with Bucky some important information of his own. "This would be the first time I've had to build a dam. My dad was caught by trappers before he could pass along his wisdom of how to do this."

With this additional disclosure, the initial tone of confrontation seems to be softening. "Sorry to hear that about your dad." Bucky says soothingly. "Maybe there is a way that we can work this out so that both of us can get what we need from a new dam and lodge."

Bucky sums up the conversation so far, "So here's where I think we are. We're both under time pressure to get this project underway. Another stream is not an option. There are some materials left over from the logging but certainly not enough for two dams. Besides, we don't want to draw attention from the townspeople by building two dams and restricting the water flow. Is that how you see the situation?"

Hardy says, "Yes, that sums it up." And adds, "We've got to resolve this quickly or the river will be flowing too fast to do any work on dams." Bucky sighs in agreement as they head back to the clearing. As they're walking, Hardy says, "Maybe its possible to build the two dams close together. That way, we'll each have our lodge and maybe it won't restrict the water flow so much."

Bucky replies "Let me think about that. Maybe our mates can help resolve this."

As they approach the clearing, Becky and Harriet join their mates in separate conversations.

Bucky says to Becky, "We just can't seem to get together on a solution that meets all of our needs."

Then, Becky says, "You mentioned yesterday that Hardy's family really can't move to another stream at this point with the new kits on the way. We don't want to move since we've been on this river for 20 years. So, how about if we offer this proposal. We could build one large dam and lodge together, and the two families could share that living space."

Bucky replies, "Interesting! That's similar to what Hardy suggested about two dams close together."

Becky continues, "It would be almost like when our kits and kitlets were still home. How I miss them! Don't you?"

Meanwhile, Hardy and Harriet are having a similar conversation. "We can't both build dams and lodges, so we have to find a compromise somehow." Hardy says.

Harriet replies, "Well, they seem like nice beavers, and it would be nice to have another family around."

Hardy says, "Let's see what Bucky and Becky have come up with."

Once they are back together, Bucky states, "I think we may have a solution. How about if we all join forces and build one large dam and lodge for all of us. What do you think?"

"How would that work?" asks Hardy.

Bucky responds, "Well, I could apply my knowledge about building a really top-notch dam, how to choose the best location as well as where to find the best materials. You could provide the muscle and energy to gather the additional branches and logs necessary for a larger dam and lodge."

A small but growing smile begins on Bucky's face. Hardy asks, "What are you grinning about?" Bucky looks at Becky, who says, "Building one large dam and lodge would also have other advantages. We've missed our kits and kitlets, and I would love to be around the new kits."

Bucky chimes in, "You have no idea how much trouble those new kits of yours will be." Now Hardy is smiling and with a slight tear in his eye says, "Ever since my dad was captured, I have been wondering how my kits could learn all the the wisdom of the older generation. I really like that idea."

Bucky summarizes, "We'll join forces and build a dam upstream on our site; and expand the size of the dam and lodge to accommodate both families. Both of us will be involved in the building; me more in the planning, and you more in gathering materials and actual construction. And, we have to move fast with the spring thaw and the new kits coming soon. Did I miss anything?"

Hardy says, "That's the agreement as I see it as well. And it's a special bonus that my family get to hear about all the things you and Becky have learned in your long lives."

Bucky and Hardy slap paddles and the deal is sealed. "Let's get to work!"

EPILOGUE:

After a brief meal to celebrate, Bucky and Hardy begin building the dam and lodge the next day. The construction takes about two weeks, just in time for the arrival of Hardy and Harriet's new kits. As the project nears completion, the environmentalist Town Council member invites the entire Town Council to inspect the site and witness the positive flow of the river waters. In addition, she points out that the dam and lodge could be a tourist attraction.

They agree to allocate some funds for a small park near the river - Beaver Dam Park. Interestingly, there is a new multipurpose mall being built nearby that would draw visitors to the park. So, the town resolves to not only preserve the dam, but to use it as a tourist attraction, build the park, and actually rename the major road nearby as Beaver Dam Road.

BEAVER DAM
PARK

ANALYSIS and COMMENTARY

Analysis

Characters (Parties):

- Older beaver, Bucky Beaver - Building dam and lodge as legacy
- Becky Beaver – Bucky's mate and key adviser
- Young beaver, Hardy Beaver - Wants to build a dam and lodge and move fast – family on the way
- Harriet Beaver – Hardy's mate and key adviser concerned about growing family
- The Town (Council) – concerned about restriction of water flow on the river and flooding.

Conflict:

- Both beavers want to build a dam and lodge on the same river for different reasons
- Due to restrictions (Town Council, water flow and materials) only ONE dam and lodge are possible.

- Competition for scarce resources
  - Time – both under time pressure
  - Materials – some felled trees left over from logging, but not enough for two dams
  - Economy of effort

Positions

- **Bucky Beaver:**
  - **Opening Position:** "I want <u>my</u> dam on this river! I've got seniority. This will be my last dam and I have to get to work on it NOW."
    - Reasons: seniority and expertise, "I've been here for 20 years", "I know how to build it."
    - Need: replace his damaged dam and lodge
    - Legacy – "my last dam".
  - **Desired Settlement Point:** a dam and lodge on this river for Bucky and Becky
  - **Walk Away:** two dams on the river
- **Hardy Beaver**
  - **Opening Position:** "I want to build <u>my</u> dam on this river. I'm young and I need a dam quickly to protect and raise my family. You're too old and slow to build a dam."
    - Reasons: Stronger and more able to build a dam and respond quickly
    - Need: housing and shelter for new family
  - **Desired Settlement Point:** a dam and lodge on this river for Hardy, Harriet and new family
  - **Walk Away:** dam on another stream

Currencies

- Knowledge of how to build a dam
- Labor to gather additional materials branches and shrubs
- Help finding another stream
- Avoiding trouble with the townspeople
- Helping to raise the new kits / family

The Agreement

- Bucky and Hardy beavers will build one large dam and lodge.
- Bucky will be responsible for siting the dam and lodge and planning the construction.
- Hardy will provide muscle to gather materials and construct the dam
- Both families will share living space.
- Bucky and Becky will be surrogate grandparents.

Commentary

This is a situation with a typical type of conflict – both parties wanting the same thing, yet seemingly only one party can win. The townspeople (represented by the Town Council) constitute a present but silent party in the negotiation. As we see from the above analysis, Bucky Beaver has a strong position, and a sense of urgency. On the other hand, Hardy Beaver has similar urgency, but less strength in his position. Urgency demands a quick solution before the river water flow increases. So, in this situation we have a combination of both common and conflicting vested interests. The common interest - the urgency to build a dam and avoid the townspeople's interference. Conflicting interest – both want a dam on **this** river.

As the situation unfolds, there is a confrontation and what appears to be an impasse. Often, this leads to an escalation of the conflict to a higher authority. If both pursue building separate dams, the Town Council (the higher authority) will have to remove one (or both) of them to ensure proper water flow to avoid flooding the roadway. This would represent a "win" for one beaver family but certainly a total loss for the other.

After explaining their positions and reaching an impasse, both parties engage in a tactic known as a **caucus** with their respective mates. Once Bucky and Hardy start to explain their positions to their mates and share information about the other beaver, we begin to explore the underlying needs of both parties as well as some currencies of exchange that might help to resolve the situation. Bucky offers the first currency of helping Hardy find another stream for his family. Even though this is unrealistic given the circumstances of Hardy's imminent family and no other viable stream, it is the first step on the bridge of trust between the parties.

The next day, when both beavers return to the river with their mates, we discover more currencies available in their respective dialogues. When Hardy shares the information about his father's demise, Bucky's experience as a seasoned dam builder becomes a highly valued currency. In addition, when Bucky acknowledges that he is tired and hopes that he has enough energy to build the dam and lodge, Hardy's youth and vigor become more valuable assets. The additional fact that Bucky and Becky could provide seasoned guidance to Hardy and Harriet in raising kits becomes both an emotional and practical currency.

The offstage presence of the Town Council provides some pressure that drives the process. In addition, with the spring thaw coming soon and more water from heavier snows, these facts provide additional urgency to the situation.

The solution of building one large dam and lodge for both families to share living space meets the underlying needs of both parties and provides an elegant resolution to the conflict.

PRACTICAL NEGOTIATING: PLANNING GUIDE and SAMPLES

Practical Negotiating: Planning Guide – *Dam It! Situation*

Planning the Negotiation between Bucky and Hardy beavers

Planning is an essential part of every negotiation. Research has proven that negotiators that engage in planning prior to the negotiation, negotiate more skillfully and effectively.

The following negotiation planning guide will help demonstrate how to use the Planning Guide. The source of this planning guide is the book *Practical Negotiating: Tools, Tactics, & Techniques* (John Wiley, 2007) by the same author. Further in this book, there is a Planning Guide which you can reproduce for your personal use.

Step 1: Determine Wants and Needs

BUCKY BEAVER SIDE	HARDY BEAVER SIDE
• What do you want? *Build a dam and lodge on the river* • What would getting this (want) do for you? *Replace his dam and lodge* *Provide shelter for family* • Is this my need? If you're not sure, ask the question again. What would getting this do for you? *Legacy – "My last dam".*	• What do they want? *Build a dam and lodge on the river* • What would getting this (want) do for them? *Provide shelter for new family* • Is this their need? If you're not sure, ask the question again. What would getting this do for them? *Prove himself as good provider and protecting his new family*

Notes: Remember that identifying and satisfying the underlying needs of both parties represents the essence of the negotiation process. Can both parties' needs be satisfied? Yes, if they explore beneath the surface. Think of some questions you might ask to surface the other side's underlying needs. Keep asking the question "What does getting this do for you?"

Needs/Objectives Matrix

Needs/Objectives	BUCKY BEAVER	HARDY BEAVER
SUBSTANTIVE	*Build a dam and lodge on the river*	*Build a dam and lodge on the river*
PERSONAL	*Build his last dam as a legacy*	*Build his first dam and demonstrate his competence to protect his new family*

Notes: To fill in these boxes, ask yourself: *What am I trying to accomplish in this negotiation?* And *What are **they** trying to accomplish?*

Answering these questions helps to identify negotiation objectives. Don't stop there. See if you can distinguish substantive and personal objectives. The substantive needs have to do with the subject of the negotiation. Ask yourself this further question: *What are my personal objectives? Theirs?* Remember the test, if you can substitute another person (on your side or theirs) and the need remains, then the need is substantive rather than personal. Review the list and circle the objectives that are most critical.

Step 2: Position Development

Notes: In a specific negotiation, needs and objectives tend to remain constant, but positions change. Every negotiation involves one or more issues. Plan a settlement range for each.   Start with a point where you think the deal can be made equitably – The Desired Settlement Point (DSP). Then, establish your Opening Position (OP), and last establish your Walkaway (WA).

BUCKY BEAVER Position Development:

Settlement Range

OP	DSP	WA
Opening Position	Desired Settlement Point	Walk Away

Issue

- "I want MY dam This river" — Dam and lodge for Bucky and Becky — Two dams on on the river
-
-

Rationale: Seniority and expertise – incumbent for 20 years. Experience in building dams.

HARDY BEAVER Position:

Settlement Range

OP	DSP	WA
Opening Position	Desired Settlement Point	Walk Away

Issue

- Build my dam on river.   Dam and lodge for his new family.   Dam on another river.

-

Rationale: Stronger and more able to build a dam and respond quickly.

Step 3: Currenies / Options

BUCKY BEAVER

> - *Knowledge of how to build a dam*
> - *Assistance in in helping Hardy find another stream*
> - *Avoiding trouble with town council*
> - *Helping to raise new kits / family*

HARDY BEAVER

> - *Labor and strength to gather materials and build the dam*
> - *Opportunity to interact with his family and forum to pass along wisdom of older/wiser beavers*

Notes: Currencies are defined as tangible or intangible resources that you control and are perceived to have value by the receiving party. Currencies are essential to the negotiation process. To determine currencies you might offer, consider what you know about the other party's needs and what currencies you might offer to meet those needs. Be sure to determine the "street value"[3] of the currencies you offer. To determine what they might offer, consider your needs and what currencies they could offer you to meet those needs.

---

[3] The term "street value" refers to the cost of securing the same good or service from another source.

Practical Negotiating: Planning Guide - For your Use

The following negotiation planning guide will help you analyze and plan for an upcoming negotiation to resolve your conflict situation. The source of this planning guide is the book *Practical Negotiating: Tools, Tactics, & Techniques* (John Wiley, 2007) by the same author. As the purchaser of this book, the author grants you permission to reproduce this planning guide for your personal use.

Step 1: Determine Wants and Needs

YOUR SIDE	OTHER SIDE
• What do you want?	• What do they want?
• What would getting this (want) do for you?	• What would getting this (want) do for them?
• Is this my need? If you're not sure, ask the question again. What would getting this do for you?	• Is this their need? If you're not sure, ask the question again. What would getting this do for them?

Notes: Remember that identifying and satisfying the underlying needs of both parties represents the essence of the negotiation process. Can both parties' needs be satisfied? Yes, if they explore beneath the surface. Think of some questions you might ask to surface the other side's underlying needs. Keep asking the question "What does getting this do for you?"

Needs/Objectives Matrix

Needs/Objectives	YOURS	OTHER SIDE
SUBSTANTIVE		
PERSONAL		

Notes: To fill in these boxes, ask yourself: *What am I trying to accomplish in this negotiation?* And *What are **they** trying to accomplish?*

Answering these questions helps to identify negotiation objectives. Don't stop there. See if you can distinguish substantive and personal objectives. The substantive needs have to do with the subject of the negotiation. Ask yourself this further question: *What are my personal objectives? Theirs?* Remember the test, if you can substitute another person (on your side or theirs) and the need remains, then the need is substantive rather than personal. Review the list and circle the objectives that are most critical.

Step 2: Position Development

Your Position Development:

Settlement Range

OP   **DSP**   **WA**

Opening Position   Desired Settlement Point   Walk Away

Issue

-
-
-

Other's Position (Speculative)

Settlement Range

OP   **DSP**   **WA**

Opening Position   Desired Settlement Point   Walk Away

Issue

-
-
-
-

Notes: In a specific negotiation, needs and objectives tend to remain constant, but positions change. Every negotiation involves one or more issues. Plan a settlement range for each. Start with a point where you think the deal can be made equitably – The Desired Settlement Point (DSP). Then, establish your Opening Position (OP), and last establish your Walkaway (WA).

Step 3: Currenies / Options

YOUR SIDE

OTHER SIDE

Notes: Currencies are defined as tangible or intangible resources that *you control* and are perceived to have value by the *receiving party.* Currencies are essential to the negotiation process. To determine currencies you might offer, consider what you know about the other party's needs and what currencies you might offer to meet those needs. Be sure to determine the "street value"[4] of the currencies you offer. To determine what they might offer, consider your needs and what currencies they could offer you to meet those needs.

Good luck in planning and conducting your next negotiation.

---

[4] The term "street value" refers to the cost of securing the same good or service from another source.

CONCLUSION

Negotiation isn't a game. It is a serious process for resolving conflict that is centered on the two parties as participants in the negotiation process rather than an external judge or authority. As we saw from this brief and simple illustration, a seemingly unresolvable conflict can be worked through and settled if both parties focus on their common interests and the needs of the other party as well as their own. Negotiation involves continuous interaction and dialogue between the parties to find a solution with maximum advantages to both sides.

In the case of Bucky, Hardy and their families, we see that continuing the dialogue and taking time away (caucusing) surfaced more information about underlying needs and potential currencies to help reach agreement. In addition, the underlying emotional component revealed needs that helped both parties realize their common interests and close the gap to creating a mutually beneficial solution.

Reaching agreement with our partners, suppliers, spouses, children, and others is not often easy. However, with a more open and sensitive approach, a more meaningful dialogue and resolution can be possible.

Good luck!

ABOUT
THE AUTHOR

Tom Gosselin brings over 35 years of international experience in developing leaders who drive organizational performance. Tom has participated in landmark research related to emotional intelligence, helping senior leaders transition in their first 90 days, and developed interventions/ coaching techniques to build emotional intelligence in executives.

Tom's book *Practical Negotiating: Tools, Tactics, and Techniques* has been hailed as "a thoughtful, engaging, and practical guide on a topic of increasing importance to leaders and organizations." In addition to his negotiation skills workshops, Tom has also been involved in several major negotiations with large clients. For instance, he has helped negotiation teams at Scripps Networks, and MTV Networks to achieve better results and develop stronger partnerships with major service operators (i.e. Verizon, Comcast, Time Warner Cable, DiSH etc.)

He has coached at all levels of organizations, from CEO to star individual contributors. Tom has served clients in: financial services, consulting and professional services, executive search, insurance, media, manufacturing, travel services, pharmaceutical and medical products, and consumer products including: Alliance Capital, Athena Health, Atrium HealthCare, Booz & Company, C.R. Bard, Ford Motor Company, Ingersoll Rand, J.P. Morgan-Chase, Johnson & Johnson, Lincoln Financial, Marsh, Mercer, McKinsey & Company, Philips, Putnam Investments, Spencer Stuart, State Street Corporation, and others.

Earlier in his career, Tom led large-scale organization development projects at MCI Telecommunications, Freddie Mac, and the US Department of Labor as a consultant with the Sterling Institute. In his work on change, Tom often leverages his previous experience as a psychotherapist in exploring organizational and interpersonal dynamics.

Tom received a BA from St. John's in Philosophy and Psychology, and an MSW from Catholic University. He also studied Organizational Behavior at George Washington University and at Boston College. Tom has been a guest lecturer on power and influence in organizations at The Harvard Business School, and he has co- designed and leads Executive Coaching Certification Programs at NYU. In addition, Tom is a trained mediator.

Contact Information:

Tom Gosselin
PRACTICAL NEGOTIATING
88 Old Field Road
Plymouth, MA 02360
617-721-4011
tom@practicalnegotiating.com